SHAME ON YOU
Breakthrough

Katina Moore Chachere Publishing

Rayne, Louisiana

2021

Katina Moore Chachere

Copyrighted Material
Shame on You Breakthrough
Copyright ©2021 by Katina Moore Chachere
All Rights Reserved.
No part of this publication may be reproduced, stored in a retrieval system, or transmitted, in any form or by any means—electronic, mechanical, photocopying, recording or otherwise—without prior written permission from the publisher, except for the inclusion of brief quotations in a review.
For information about this title or to order other books and/or electronic media, contact the publisher:
Katina Moore Chachere
Publisher email: Tinamoechachere@gmail.com
ISBN: 9780578882970
Printed in the United States of America
Cover design: Mde Films
Interior and layout design:
Donica Strange Reescano
C.U.T.E Self-Publishing and Writing Consultation
iamdonica@gmail.com
Publisher's Cataloging-In-Publication Data: available upon request
Scripture references courtesy of
Scripture quotations marked NIV are taken from the Holy Bible, New International Version® Copyright © 1973, 1978, 1984, 2011 by Biblica Inc.™ Used by permission of Zondervan. All rights reserved worldwide. www.zondervan.com. The "NIV" and "New International Version" are trademarks registered in the United States Patent and Trademark by Biblica, Inc.™
King James Version by use of public domain.

CONTENTS

Shame on You Breakthrough

PREFACE

1	LEARNING TO FAST	i
2	ACKNOWLEDGEMENTS	V
3	FOREWORD	5
4	INTRODUCTION	7
6	KATINA'S JOURNEY	9
7	KATINA'S PRAYER	13
8	FASTING JOURNEY	17
9	BREAKTHROUGH YOUR JOURNEY	21
10	PRAYER JOURNEY	37
11	AFTERWORD	45
12	REFERENCES	47
13	ABOUT THE AUTHOR	54

PREFACE

Stop! Before you start the journey of reading this book written by Katina Moore Chachere, one must know and understand this is a spiritual journey. A journey which God has taken Katina on to receive the healing deliverance and breakthrough she was seeking. I beseech you to put on your spiritual lens and ask God to give you the spiritual insight you need.

This is a powerful book that shares a message of deliverance from addiction. Millions of Americans struggle with drug addiction. They are often without support hope love or even a home. As the Opioid crisis was raging in America, the drug epidemic was also raging in the heart and life of Katina. She found the answer to her problem.

The answer is a spiritual one. The answer is the same one Nicodemus sought when he went to Jesus Christ in the middle of the night – salvation. Unless we are born again, we cannot see the kingdom of God. We cannot see the deliverance and breakthrough we desire. One must repent - turn away from our sins. In the book of Acts chapter 2, it says, "Repent and be baptized every one of you, in the name of Jesus Christ for the remission of your sins. And ye shall receive the gift of the Holy Spirit." We must believe change is possible. We speak of what we know and what we have seen. This is the theme weaved in this book. A story of salvation. We see it in the life of Katina.

Katina shares her salvation story. Her salvation story includes her testimony, dreams and visions God gave her. The book provides the process Katina endured to get HER breakthrough. Finally, it culminates with a prayer for you the reader. Join Katina NOW! Her breakthrough is for you too.

Donica Strange Reescano

Author Coach

C.U.T.E Self-Publishing and Writing Consultation

LEARNING TO FAST

Fasting is a spiritual process which helps you grow biblically and spiritually. Fasting is to abstain from food. Great modern leaders, historic, and biblical leaders have taught us about fasting through example and teaching. Biblical leader and teacher Derrick Prince defined fasting as "voluntarily abstaining from food for spiritual purposes". The late Dr. Myles Munroe defined fasting as "a conscious, intentional decision to abstain for a time from the pleasure of eating in order to gain vital spiritual benefits". To understand the nature of fasting we must know the types of fasts.

Types of Fasts

- Normal – Abstaining from food.
- Absolute – Abstaining from food and water. An absolute fast should not be undertaken longer than three days. You must be under the direction of a physician.
- Juice – Intaking fruit and vegetable juices only.
- Partial Fast – Abstaining from certain types of food. An example of this is a Daniel Fast. In Daniel 10:3 Daniel said, "I ate no pleasant bread, neither came flesh nor wine in my mouth, neither did I anoint myself at all, till three whole weeks were fulfilled".
- Corporate Fast – Group of people fast together for a certain cause at a specific time.

These fasts offer different types of spiritual fasts. It is important that we realize that there are other reasons to fast or abstain from food. The connection in spiritual fasting as Dr. Munroe said is to "gain vital spiritual benefits" is your spiritual connection through prayer, scripture reading, and abstinence. The absence of these connectors is just refraining from eating.

Abstaining for Health & Wellness

Biometric Screenings

When you go to your physician's office, they draw blood from you for your biometric screening. Prior to your physician appointment, the nurse or medical assistant provides you with treatment instructions. Those instructions advise you to fast from nine to twelve hours prior to your screening. This fast provides a more accurate read out of your biometric results.

Surgeries

Physicians and anesthesiologists require patients to refrain from foods and liquids at least six hours prior to surgery.

Intermittent Fasting

Intermittent Fasting is a wellness strategy which requires the individual to voluntarily fast for a specific period. This approach allows eating and abstaining from eating in cycles over a specific time frame. This fast's benefits are health and wellness such as weight loss and improving overall health.

As you can see, fasting offers benefits that are health related, supports surgical efficacy, and in some cases, we just missed a meal because we were busy. The difference between these forms of abstaining from food and spiritual fasting is a spiritual focus.

Prayer

Prayer is a form of spiritual focus which connects us to God. Prayer is communication with God. Prayer allows you to hear from God and focus on the message he is communicating to you during your focus of fasting. Isaiah 58:6 says, "Is not this the fast that I choose: to lose the bonds of wickedness, to undo the straps of the yoke, to let the oppressed go free, and to break every yoke?" Just as Katina has written, fasting breaks yokes. Nehemiah said when he fasted, he prayed. *"When I heard these words, I sat down and wept and mourned for days; and I was fasting and praying before the God of heaven."* **(Nehemiah 1:1-4)**

Scripture Reading

Joshua 1:8 says, "This book of the law shall not depart out of thy mouth; but thou shalt meditate therein day and night, that thou mayest observe to do according to all that is written therein: for then thou shalt make thy way prosperous, and then thou shalt have good success."

Abstinence

During our fast, we must turn off the things of the world to clearly connect with God. That may mean abstaining from social media, television, socializing with friends, or abstaining from something that is very important to us. This area of abstinence allows time to pray, read scriptures, and have a time of meditation. Our day to day lives are filled with many carnal messages. Removing these messages is going to open our heart and ears to hear from God.

Biblical Examples of Fasting

- The disciples Fasted - Matthew 17:21
- Ezra Fasted - Ezra 8:21 – 23
- Samuel fasted - I Sam 7:6
- Elijah fasted -I King 19: 4- 8
- John The
- Baptist fasted – Luke 7:33 - 35
- Daniel fasted – Daniel 10:3
- Jesus fasted – Mark 1:13; Matthew 4:1–11; Luke 4:1–13

Fasting is our method to grow biblically and spiritually. Understanding the differences between abstaining and a spiritually connected fast will help the believer grow. This growth brings about breakthrough and deliverance. You deserve to have the God ordained breakthrough he has for your life. Seek Him through fasting today.

Monica Strange, MA
Author
The Recovery Evangelist

ACKNOWLEDGEMENTS

I would like to express my special thanks and gratitude to my Lord and Savior Jesus Christ. I do not know where I would be without my King of Kings.

Thank you to my Pastor Jared Pavlv and your family for all your sweet prayers and hugs. May God keep pouring His love into you to pour in us. My Point Church family thank you for all the beautiful hugs and the love you give. You have a caring spirit that cannot be found anywhere else. Thank you. May God keep using you and keep being available.

Sister Nicole thank you so much my sister for pushing me on my journey with God. You are like a real sister to me always available when I call. May God give you a double portion in this season just for the waiting. May God keep showing Himself strong in your life and your family.

Sister Mary thank you for being such a sweetheart in my life. Thank you for allowing God to use you to always have the right words to encourage me and get me happy in the Holy Ghost. We have so much laughter and tears together. Thank you and your family for always letting the Lord use you. When you can be anywhere else you rather be in the house of the Lord. May God keep using you and your family to pour his love on others.

Sister Liz thank you for always letting God use you to tell them demons "not today." Thank you, sister of warfare, may God continue to pour his love on you and your family. Go get them souls sister.

Sister Jessica you are so humble and full of jokes. You are an inspiration on your spiritual warfare. Thank you, may God use you to tear down walls that no one in your family did.

Sister Shannon always smiling and in the same mood all the time. Thank you for always giving them sweet hugs and encouraging words. May God pour back into you everything you pour into others.

Sister Catherine such a powerful teacher of God. I am so thankful for you because it is so many times, I need a word and God will use you to deliver it. Sometimes you did not know He was rebuking me too. Thank you for always being available. May the good Lord pour everything you sow back into your children and grandchildren.

Sister Ella and the Handy family I miss you so much. I miss seeing your beautiful faces. You know God's sheep when you speak to the children of God always providing encouraging words. You all know the parts you played in my life. Thank you so much. May God continue to use each one of you.

Sister Deeon you are like another mother. If I need anything, I can call you. Even with prayers you are always available. There were times I felt uncertain, and the Lord would use you to call me. I am so very thankful for a special person like you. May our king pour back into you everything the devil stole from you.

Sister Lanita such a sweetheart. It is so sweet how we met but God does not make mistakes. I love you my sister. Thank you for always being a phone call away. May my Father shower you with blessings that you will not have room to handle for you and my babies.

Tamarcus my love bug I would not trade you for nothing in this world. I remember the first thing you told me when we met. You said, "That's my wife" and you did not stop until you had me. Proverbs 18:22 "He who finds a wife finds what is good and receives favor from the Lord." Thank you, my love, for always reminding me I can do it no matter how many times I fall. I love you my King. May God pour wisdom knowledge on you and understanding that you can go into all the earth and use it.

Keyshawn my lil baby. I miss those beautiful hugs and kisses. You would creep in the room and give me a kiss or a hug and say, "Mom I love you." Thank you, God, for using my son to pray for me when I was lost in the streets and did not know who to turn to. Keyshawn you said, "Mom I put your name in the prayer box at church today." May our Lord Jesus Christ hear every prayer you have stored up in the bottle. May this year overflow with blessings for you and your children. I love you Mackenzie and Zander and Lil Keyshawn.

Dayonna when I first saw those beautiful eyes of yours, I fell in love with you. You have such a big heart. I love how you always have a smile on your face no matter what you are going through. Nobody can take your smile away from you. I love you daughter. May my King pour the world on you. The sky is the limit. Philippians 4:13 "I can do all things through Christ who strengtheneth me." You can do it!

Yvonne thank you so much for being you - my mom. You are someone I always wanted to be like. Words cannot explain how much I love you. I am so thankful for you teaching me how God is real, and nobody will love me like God. I pray God pour a double portion of His gifts of the spirit in your life for the pain and suffering.

Shantel thanks my dear sister for always reminding me it is okay to fall and get back up. "Do it again Tina," I hear you saying. I would not trade you for anything big sister. I love and adore you for being a friend and sister a counsellor and a mentor all in one. Wisdom, CJ, and Shawn this is your season for you to receive the overflow and a new beginning. So, get ready sis.

Keysuana my queen my baby. I love you Key you are so sweet, and you will give me the shirt off your back too. Keep your big sister happy. Key, the SKY is the limit for you my love. You can do it sis, get back up. Use the tools you have. God got you sister.

Larry my big brother my protector "Lil sister I got you," you always say, "you don't have to worry." I thank God for my big brother. "That is my Daddy," we say about you. I love you Bro, God got you. "Be strong and courageous. Do not be afraid or terrified because of them, for the Lord your God goes with you, he will never leave you or forsake you." (Deuteronomy 31:6).

Courtney my baby brother my ride with me until the wheels fall off. You always say, "I got you big sis." I am so thankful for the man you are becoming. God is not done with you yet. The best is yet to come brother.

Jacory I miss you. I miss you dearly. We do not know what our work is going to be here on earth. All I can tell you my lil brother is God will never give us more than we can bare. Keep being faithful. One day you will hear, "Well done." I love you Jay!

Kim and Brittany, Nanny, my sweet sisters I love you! I cannot thank God enough for how much you prayed for me. Thank you for the late-night calls telling me, "It's just warfare. You are going to be okay." Thank you for always pushing me when I am weak. May my heavenly father pour back into you everything you pour into others -double for your troubles. He will give you whatever your heart desires.

The Rogers, Pastor Mike and Pastor Cheryl thank you so much for the lifting up every Tuesday. Thank God for your faithfulness. You are like a mother and father to me Thank you so much. I am glad to have you in my life. May God continue to use you mightily in this earth and send many souls for you to pour into.

Sister Sally you are such a sweetheart. You always speak the truth in my life. You constantly remind me to fight. You tell me to not give up. I pray God bless you with double for your trouble for all the years you did not give up on God. You are a warrior that stood through all the storms. Watching the fight in you keeps me fighting.

Donica and Monica thank God for you too. It is a short moment of knowing you but what I do know of you two I take you in already as family. Thank you so much for being a part of writing this book and being available for God to use you. This is your winning season and everybody around you will win.

Moore's Malbrough's Chachere's Carrier's Guidry's every one of my family members I love you. Be blessed. God loves you.

Proverbs 31 Women I thank God for each one of you for your prayers and encouragement. I pray God meet your every need and allow you to grow in wisdom and knowledge. I love you.

Katina Moore Chachere

FOREWORD

Tamarcus Chachere is Katina's husband of 8 years.

Katina is my backbone, best friend my go to and my supporter. We met in 2006. Years later, we began our journey together as a couple. On November 29, 2013, we were married and became one. Still today we are on our journey. I am writing today to inform you because I witnessed my wife overcoming addiction. She has committed her life unto God's will and purpose. She is a great mother and the most amazing wife. In this book you will learn and experience, the steps (she used) to overcoming addiction. Her step-by-step process and how my wife overcame something that looking on the outside seems impossible to do. I have learned from her step-by-step process that overcoming anything, not just addiction, can be done if you are determined to become the person who God created you to be.

Tamarcus V. Chachere

INTRODUCTION

I Katina Moore Chachere was a slave to addictions for a long time. I was in captivity and bondages. I was broken from some things. I also was consumed by fear. I was ashamed of myself. When you are in bondage you have blinders on your eyes. You cannot see where you are going in life. I allowed my addictions to keep me enslaved in a little box – not understanding it was spiritual.

As a youth, I was molested by a female relative. Years later I went to her and told her about what she did to me and I forgive her and release her. This is a part of my breakthrough story and I believe it is necessary for me to share so others can get the deliverance they need by reading my story. I have gone through many things, but I knew God had the answer.

I never realized I needed a breakthrough. When I turned to God, I got my breakthrough. God can do the same for you. He is the same God. All you need to do is fast and pray. He waits on us to take our hands out of the situation and surrender. I surrendered to the Most-high and he broke chains off my life.

I am a living witness nobody told me this. I walked this lifestyle, and I overcame by the blood of the lamb and the word of my testimony. I lived a life in shame and fear. I worried that I would die in shame. This is my story for the Lord's glory. My family was praying for me to be set free and you know what their prayers were not in vain.

I got baptize in Jesus' name for the remission of my sins. I am no longer a slave to addiction. I am renewed in my mind. I look different, I speak different. I am more positive about myself. I no longer live with fear or shame. My family and friends say I look different now. I do not have the same friends. The song says I know I have been changed. I can focus more on life.

My daddy is a living proof. He was in addiction also. For years he cried for help. The Lord came and helped him, and he turned from his wicked ways. He allowed God to mold him. My son is a living witness he started running in and out of jail. He got hooked on drugs, but he has been healed and set free. My husband is a living witness to selling drugs and going back and forth to jail. I have seen many miracles in people's lives. I am a miracle. We all are curse breakers. We must keep crying out to God and when He comes; take the invitation.

Jesus' promises are Yes and amen. He is not a man that he should lie. He is not a respecter of person. If He did it for me, He will do it for you. His word says try me and see. He is the God that will set you free. He is our beginning and end. He knows everything and he knows what we all need. Try Jesus!

You need to get this book as soon as possible. It is going to set you free. Do not delay. Do not get it and lay it on your shelves or put it down in the car or table. Make sure you tell a friend or somebody. This book will change your life. Make sure you read it to the end. This is how you get your breakthrough. Go get it now! You will not regret it.

KATINA'S JOURNEY

When the Lord told me to write this book, I was still trying to break free from so many chains such as, brokenness, heartbreak, the spirit of fear and worries, fatigue all the time, stress, and different emotions. But the love of God can do all things. Thank you, God, for being so merciful and loveable. In the present times, I realized to just trust in the Lord and not in man, but the Lord. For instance, do not put your trust in your children, but in God always. It is so sweet to rest in the Lord's presence and to know Him for ourselves. God is really our first love over everything.

God is my miracle worker, my King of Kings and Lord of Lords. It is the Lord's timing in our lives when we are so tired that we do not have a choice, but to love on the Lord. Sometimes everybody we turn to will turn their backs on us. If we have tried many things, now we must look to God for everything. At this point, we are going to Him with all our tears and our brokenness because He is the only one that can love us back together and give us the strength to keep going.

People always say, "I am going to always love you," but they do not. It is okay because we all fail God with something. I love how He never leaves us nor forsakes us. We are the ones that have forsaken Him. Thank God for His mercy that is new to me every day. With that being said, we are limited to what we know - people are not in control; God is in control. The way He wants things to turn out for our lives is for our benefit. Sometimes God wants our attention you know when we call God will leave the 99 to chase the one, so give it all to Him.

Other times, we get so tired, and we say, "God have all of me." We stop running and fighting ourselves and Him. It is so easy to give up and let Him have his way with us. His way is the best. When we are brokenhearted and the only one who can heal us is the King of Kings and Lord of Lords, so we run straight to Him. Everybody handles things differently. Some of us start smoking. Some drink. Others gamble. Yes, and some of us do other things, but God! We can try everything in this world nobody or nothing can kill that thirst as the Lord can.

I tried all these things and all it did was made it worse for me. I was a drug head for 6 years. I took pain pills. I smoked cigarettes like they were a train back and forth. The Lord woke me up one night when I was in a deep sleep from taking Adderall and a pain pill together. The Lord told me that the devil was trying to kill my son. I asked the Lord what I should do. Then I found out that one of my friend's mom overdosed on pain pills. This scared the Joe Joe out of me. I started crying out to the Lord. Maybe two days later, I heard a loud noise on the road, so I thought I was awake, but I was sleeping, and the Lord asked me to pray.

I did not know how to pray but I started praying for the man driving the trash truck (the noise I heard on the road.) Then I asked the Lord, "Father why do people do witchcraft?" and he said to pray. When I woke up, I opened the bible. God led me to the verse saying that the Lord created good and evil. Yes, He gives us all free will to do good or evil. The next day I went on my journey with me and Jesus.

The Lord led me on a seven-day fast to drink water for 12 hours - 7 am until 7 pm. "But this kind of demon does not go out except by prayers and fasting." (Matthew 17:21.) I did not eat anything until 7 pm. The Lord delivered me on the 7th day. I was delivered and set free from pain pills after a 6-year addiction. "If the son therefore shall make you free, ye shall be free indeed." (John 8:36.) "I can do all things through Christ who strengtheneth me." (Philippians 4:13.)
I prayed the prayers the Lord led me to pray. I would sing it in my spirit. I kept encouraging myself. On day seven of my fast, I was filled with the Holy Spirit. I learned that we try to do things on our own.

In conclusion, we try to do things like delivering ourselves from drugs and smoking and other things. Everything the Lord does is well done. We mess things up. Only through His grace and mercy we receive the breakthrough we desire. I want to encourage someone that is trying to be free from things. I want you to know the Lord has everything you need.

KATINA'S PRAYER

Hallelujah Hallelujah Hallelujah
I thank you Father
I thank you Father
I give you glory Jesus
I give you praise oh God
I worship you
I Adore You Lord
I come to you as humbly as I know how oh God
Asking you to forgive me for my sins Father God
for the ones I know and the ones I don't know Father God
I come to you Father God with decree and declare anything that has been spoken over my life that is not of you oh God
I thank you that you send an angel to go into the spiritual room right now Father God
And to go to war for me Lord
that any word curses that has been spoken to me since my youth…
I thank you Lord that you bound it up and send it back to the pits of Hell
Any word curses spoken over me oh God
I thank you right now Father God that my angel goes before me and bind it up and sends it back to the sea from which it comes from in the name of Jesus
I send down in consuming fire any words that has been manifest over my life. oh God
Any words spoken oh God I am ugly, that I'm not a child of God that I will die. I will die prematurely.
Any word that has been spoken that I would be a pill head that I will be addicted to anything.
I thank you Lord that those words with burn in the fire of the Holy Ghost Father God and Father God go back to the pits of hell
No word curse that has been spoken will Manifest oh God
You said, "What I bind on Earth shall be bound in heaven."
You said, "What I loose on Earth shall be loosed in heaven."
Father God I thank you Lord God that you will demand any word curse that has been spoken on me…

Shame on You Breakthrough

I am a child of God
I am fearfully and wonderfully made.
I am bold as a lion
You are my king and my Alpha and Omega oh God
I will lack nothing in the world oh God.
You say Father God, "You will supply all my needs according to your riches and glory in Christ Jesus."
You said Father God that you knew me in my mother's womb.
I thank you Father God anything that has been spoken since I was in my mother's womb, I thank you Father God its burn into the sea from which it comes from in the name of Jesus
You said, "Power is in the tongue."
Anybody that has spoken anything over me Father God. I dismantle it!
Thank you, God, that I can have life in all areas of my life
I shall live in all areas
Thank you that every word spoken over me that is not of You is burning in the fire of the sea
I am free!
You said, "Who the son has set free, is free indeed."
I thank you for liberty
I thank you Father
I thank you my King of Kings and Lord of Lords
I give you praise
I give you glory
I give you honor
I call it done oh God
Not my will but your perfect will
I thank you Holy Ghost fire

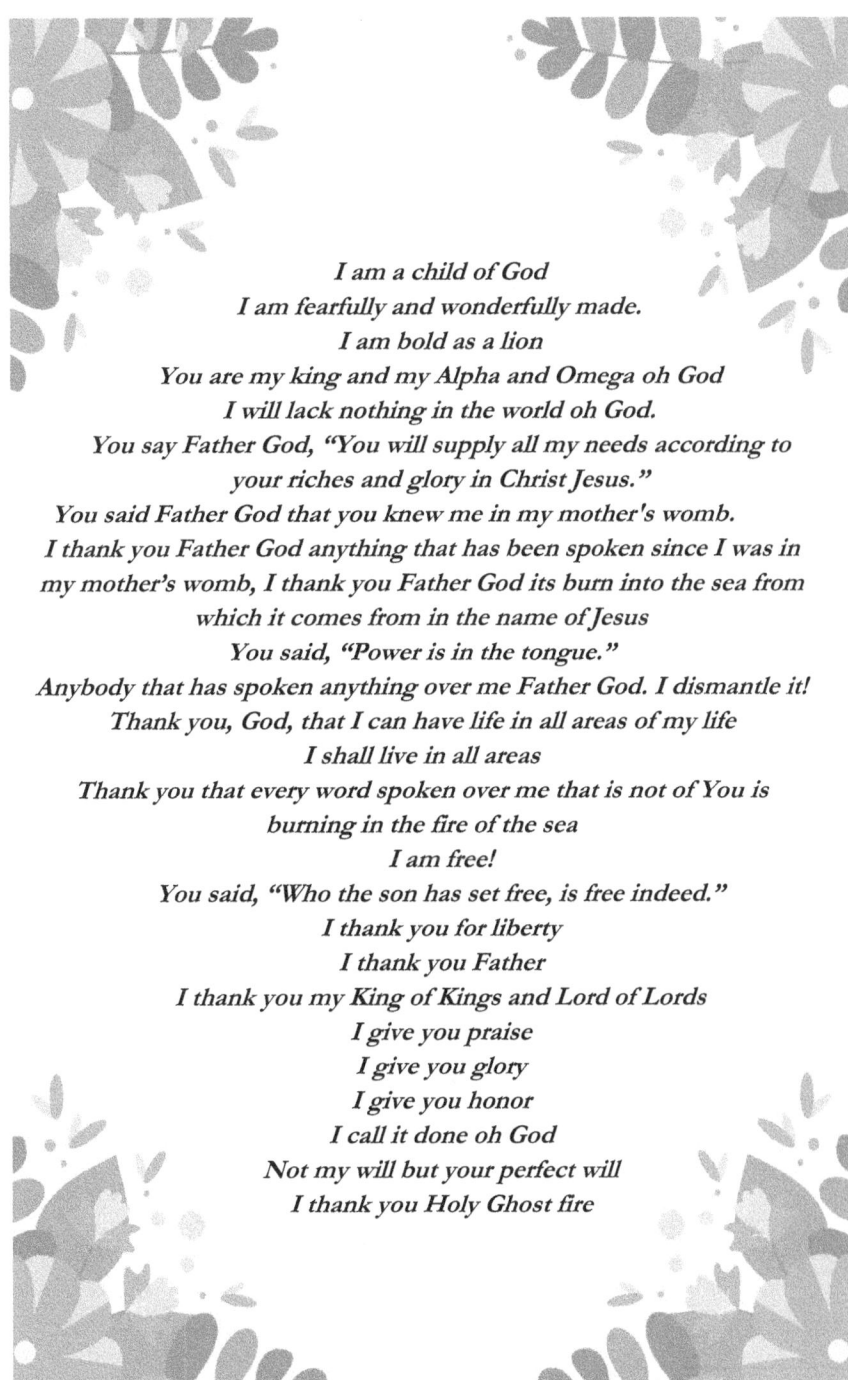

FASTING JOURNEY

When I was on pills for 6 years, I heard a friend overdosed on pain pills, so I started to cry out to God. I was so afraid it would be me next. I read Psalm 70 for years not knowing it is a prayer of deliverance. I remember the day I took a pain pill and an Adderall together. I went to bed crying to God saying, "Do not let me die like this. People going to laugh at me. Do not let me die in shame." So that night I went into a deep sleep and I heard this voice say, "Pray." I did not know it was the Lord, but I started praying. I heard a trash truck in the yard not knowing I was still sleeping, and I said, "Lord why do people do witchcraft?" I heard the Lord say, "Pray" so I start praying for the man driving the trash truck. "Lord protect this man from evil and wicked people in this world and lord protect his family." Then I woke up.

I woke up, looked outside my trash was still there, so I was like "Wow." Then I went back to my room. I remember asking the Lord, "Why do people do witchcraft and stuff?" Then he led me to Isaiah 45:7, "I form the light and create darkness I make and create evil..." Then he told me, "I give everyone free will." It means that although God made the world, and it was good it is up to humans whether they choose to do good or bad deeds.

The Holy Spirit led me to fast for 7 days. I fasted 7am to 7pm. I only drank water until 7pm then I ate what I liked. He sent me to Matthew 6:16 "Moreover when ye fast, be not, as the hypocrites, of a sad countenance for they disfigure their faces, that they may appear unto men to fast. Verily I say unto you, They have their reward." Then I was guided by the Holy spirit to read Matthew 17:21 "Howbeit this kind goeth not out but by prayer and fasting." **This is the first day on my journey for fasting for 7 days.**

Day 2 of my fasting journey - I went into a deep sleep and I thought, "Lord, where am I?" Then I noticed it was hot and dark. I started crying. I am in shock crying, "Jesus, where am I?" Then, I see a bright light. It was so beautiful. I heard the voice say Psalm 139:8 "If

I ascend upon heaven, thou art there if I make my bed in hell behold, thou art there." Then the voice said read, Acts 2:35 "Until I make thy foes thy footstool." I remember waking up saying, "I walked through hell, but the Lord saved me." I also read Philippians 4:13 "I can do all things through Christ who strengtheneth me." I quote this all day in my spirit and, I spoke it out loud and drank water until 7pm. **This is the second day on my journey for fasting for 7 days.**

Day 3 of my fasting journey - I fell into a deep sleep. Again, all I saw was my body lying there. My spirit leaving my body going up. I heard this voice, nobody but God, say, "put her down." Then I knew the devil and his demons were trying to kill me, but God said, "No." I remember waking up in stock thinking "Lord what happened?" Then I heard the Lord say there was a man in my house by my bed and another one by the window. "*What?*" I thought. But they could not touch me. Exodus 14:14 NIV says, "The Lord will fight for you all you need only to be still." **This is the third day on my journey for fasting for 7 days.**

Day 4 of my fasting journey - I keep hearing things in my house. On day four, I was in so much fear. But 1 Timothy 1:7 "For God hath not given us the spirit of fear but of power and of love and of a sound mind." Something was scratching on the door in my house. I called my mom saying, "Can you call someone to pray my house out? They have so many demons in my house." Then I just kept saying in my spirit "*I can do all things through Christ who strengtheneth me.*" Their job was to put me in so much fear until I will take a pain pill. That day I drank water until 7pm. And I prayed. **This is the fourth day on my journey for fasting for 7 days.**

Day 5 of my fasting journey - the Lord showed me how people speak word curses over each other and over themselves. Words have life. People sit under trees and speak curses. They speak words like "I hate this person and I wish she would die." Others say, "These children are going to kill me." The Lord told me to break word curses off me and my family. By praying every word curse that has been spoken over my life, I sent it back to the pits of hell in Jesus' name. Proverbs 18:21 "Death and life are in the power of the tongue and they that love it shall eat the fruit of it." I drank water all day until 7pm. I was singing in my spirit "I can do all things through Christ who strengtheneth me." **This is the fifth day on my journey for fasting for 7 days.**

Day 6 of my fasting journey - the Lord woke me up out of my sleep. I went beside my bed and I got on my knees. A man came and I opened my hand, and he gave me something. He had a sweet smell. He was wearing gold and white clothes. It was so beautiful that day. I remember I was praying and thanking God and I started speaking in tongues. Then the Spirit told me my tongues was saying, "I will watch what I speak." I was filled with the Holy Ghost at home. I still believe today the man was an angel, and he brought the gift of the Holy Spirit to me. Acts 2:4 "And they were all filled with the Holy Ghost and began to speak with other tongues as the Spirit gave them utterance." I drank water until 7pm that day and spoke in tongues and sang "I can do all things through Christ who strengtheneth me." **This is the sixth day on my journey for fasting for 7 days.**

Day 7 of my fasting journey - I went to Point Church in Church point LA. I was baptized in Jesus' name. I will never forget it was the day before my birthday. Acts 2:38 "Then Peter said unto them Repent and be baptized every one of you in the name of Jesus Christ for the remission of sins and ye shall receive the gift of the Holy Ghost." The last day I drank water until 7 pm. I was singing in my spirit and speaking in tongues, and the Lord led me to Matthew 17:20 "And Jesus said unto them, Because of your unbelief: for verily I say unto you, if ye have faith as a grain a of mustard seed, ye shall say unto this mountain, Remove hence to yonder place; and it shall remove, and nothing shall be impossible for you." I always remember if I am going to fast, I must have prayers with it. Or it is just a diet. **This is the seventh day on my journey for fasting for 7 days.**

BREAKTHROUGH YOUR JOURNEY

DAY 1 – OBEDIENCE

Obedience -Compliance with an order, request, or law or submission to another's (God's) authority.

Matthew 17:21 "Howbeit this kind goeth not out but by prayer and fasting."

In the journey of fasting, I learned to obey the voice of God. When God asked me to begin my fast, I was still struggling with my pill addiction, but I obeyed. In your journey of fasting and the journey of life, you must learn to obey God no matter the cost.

Write about an incident that is leading you to seek your breakthrough. The thing you are obeying the voice of God to receive your deliverance.

_____

_____

_____

_____

_____

_____

_____

Document your success in the Lord here, or even your struggles or failure as you continue to obey God.

_____

_____

_____

_____

Day 1 Obedience continued

Read these verses on obedience: John 14:23, Proverbs 6:20, Deuteronomy 28:1, Deuteronomy 5:33, Romans 12:2, Romans 5:19, I Kings 2:3, Joshua 1:8, Psalm 128:1

Write a prayer of obedience to the Lord in your own words:

_____

_____

_____

_____

_____

_____

Observe what the LORD your God requires: Walk in obedience to him, and keep his decrees and commands, his laws, and regulations, as written in the Law of Moses. Do this so that you may prosper in all you do and wherever you go. I Kings 2:3 NIV

Day 2 - STRENGTH

Philippians 4:13 "I can do all things through Christ who strengthened me."

During Day 2 of my fast and throughout my journey, I quoted this verse all day. Do you believe Christ to strengthened you? Write now

_____

_____

_____

_____

_____

_____

_____

Document your success in the Lord here, or even your struggles or failure as you allow God to give you strength.

_____

_____

_____

_____

Day 2 Strength continued

Write a prayer asking God to give you strength.

_____

_____

_____

_____

Day 3 –

THE LORD WILL FIGHT FOR YOU

Exodus 14:14 NIV "The Lord will fight for you all you need only to be still."

This is a spiritual battle that you are in. You are in the fighting in the spirit, but you need to know that the Lord will fight the battle for you. This does not mean you do not have to do anything, but it means He is fighting for you. In the third day of my fast God showed me He was fighting for me. God is fighting for you too.

Write a declaration declaring that God is fighting for you and everything in your life…And receive that declaration over your life.

Write now…

_____

_____

_____

_____

_____

_____

_____

Day 3 The Lord Will Fight for You continued

Document your success in the Lord here, or even your struggles or failure as you trust and know God is fighting for you.

_____

_____

_____

_____

Write a prayer of praise thanking God for fighting the battle for you on this journey.

_____

_____

_____

_____

He says, "Be still, and know that I am God;
I will be exalted among the nations,
I will be exalted in the earth." Psalm 46:10

Day 4 – Courageous

1 Timothy 1:7 "For God hath not given us the spirit of fear but of power and of love and of a sound mind."

Make a list of reasons you need courage in your life.

_____

_____

_____

_____

_____

_____

_____

Document your success in the Lord here, or even your struggles or failure on day four as you continue to be courageous on your journey.

_____

_____

_____

_____

Day 4 Courageous continued

Write a prayer asking God to increase your courage and remove any fears.

_____

_____

_____

_____

Shame on You Breakthrough

Day 5 - WORD BLESSINGS

Proverbs 18;21 "Death and life are in the power of the tongue and they that love it will eat its fruit."

So many times, in your life you have cursed yourself, your life, your children, and those things important to you. Today that will stop! Cover your life with blessings. Cover your life with peace. How? Your own words bring blessings. First start with a place of repentance. "Oh, he's lazy." Or, maybe you said, "My son or daughter won't be anything". Repent now! Write a prayer of repentance for those times you said words that were really curses.

_____

_____

_____

_____

_____

_____

_____

Day 5 Word Blessings continued

Document your success in the Lord here, or even your struggles or failure on day five of your journey.

_____

_____

_____

_____

Word Blessings.......

Now write a prayer of blessings over yourself, your family, your ministry, your business, your health, and all those things important to you. Write bold, positive, and anointed words which involve the anointed covering of God that you have and deserve.

_____

_____

_____

_____

Day 6 - BELIEVE

Philippians 4:13 "I can do all things through Christ who strengthened me."

On day 6 of your journey, what are you believing God for? Write now

_____

_____

_____

_____

_____

_____

Document your success in the Lord here, or even your struggles or failure on day six of your journey

_____

_____

_____

_____

Day 6 Believe continued

Write a prayer of praise thank God for His many blessings in your life.

_____

_____

_____

_____

Day 7 FAITH

Matthew 17:20 "And Jesus said unto them, Because of your unbelief: for verily I say unto you, if ye have faith as a grain of mustard seed, ye shall say unto this mountain, Remove hence to yonder place; and it shall remove, and nothing shall be impossible for you."

How has your faith carried you on this journey?

_____

_____

_____

_____

_____

_____

Document your success in the Lord here, today is day seven. You made it!

_____

_____

_____

_____

Day 7 Faith continued

Write a prayer asking God to allow you to walk in continual faith.

_____

_____

_____

_____

Shame on You Breakthrough

PRAYER JOURNEY

As you continue your breakthrough journey, in the next coming days and weeks uses these pages to journal your prayers to God.

_____

_____

_____

_____

_____

_____

_____

_____

_____

_____

_____

_____

_____

_____

_____

PRAYER JOURNEY

PRAYER JOURNEY

PRAYER JOURNEY

PRAYER JOURNEY

PRAYER JOURNEY

_____

_____

_____

_____

_____

_____

_____

_____

_____

_____

_____

_____

_____

_____

PRAYER JOURNEY

AFTERWORD

My name is Shantel Small. I am Katina's older sister. First, I am very proud of my sister's recovery and her relationship with God. My sister is such a beautiful person, amazing mother, and a Proverbs 31 wife to her husband.

I did not realize my sister had a substance abuse addiction until she was delivered and set free. Katina hid her substance abuse addiction very well, I believe. For example, I did not observe her showing signs of someone under the influence or a person addicted to drugs. She called me one morning in April 2015; she explained she dreamt about walking around hell. She stated one of our relatives had given her some pills and told her not to overdose on the number of pills. At that point, I realized my sister was addicted to pills. She explained that she had been addicted to pills for years. She expressed that she believed she was healed last night. I remembered after that morning, I observed her discussing God and the Bible more. Katina stopped isolating herself, she changed her appearance, and attended church every day. Katina would talk to anyone around the neighborhood about God and she would share her testimony. I observed her hunger for God's word and to have a deeper relationship with God. She had a joy and glow about her as though she was a pregnant woman. Due to my educational background of treatments and addictions, I kept wondering if she was having any cravings. I thought she needed to complete substance abuse treatment to cease from her addiction. BUT God showed us that Jesus died on the cross for Katina's healing and deliverance.

My dad was an alcoholic for over 20 years and on one Sunday he decided to quit drinking alcohol and smoking. He accepted Jesus Christ as his Lord and Savior that day. My dad did not seek any substance abuse treatment to stop drinking alcohol and smoking cigarettes. He remained sober for 15 years. I believe my dad broke the curse for my sister to be set free as the same year my sister was set free in April 2015; my dad died the same year in November 2015. I believe that God speaks to us with numbers; my dad died 7 months later after my sister was healed. The number 7 means completion and believed my sister was completely healed like my dad suddenly be healed from alcohol abuse. Although, my sister grieved the sudden death of our father; she continued trusting in God and she did not relapse.

I want to encourage anyone struggling with alcohol addiction or any substance addiction; God can heal you suddenly and set you free as he did for my sister and my dad. I have observed the behavioral change with dad & sister. My sister & dad turned their cravings towards the word of God and God can do the same for you. Please allow my sister's book to witness to you and encourage you that God is still a healer, deliverer, way maker, and the real treatment for all sorts of addictions.

I am so proud of you sis and you modeling the way for others be healed!
I love you so much, Proverbs 31 Woman!

REFERENCES

Luke 15:3-7

³ And he spake this parable unto them, saying,

⁴ What man of you, having an hundred sheep, if he lose one of them, doth not leave the ninety and nine in the wilderness, and go after that which is lost, until he find it?

⁵ And when he hath found it, he layeth it on his shoulders, rejoicing.

⁶ And when he cometh home, he calleth together his friends and neighbours, saying unto them, Rejoice with me; for I have found my sheep which was lost.

⁷ I say unto you, that likewise joy shall be in heaven over one sinner that repenteth, more than over ninety and nine just persons, which need no repentance.

Proverb 18:21
Death and life are in the power of the tongue: and they that love it shall eat the fruit thereof.

Isaiah 45:7
I form the light, and create darkness: I make peace, and create evil: I the LORD do all these things.

Matthew 6:16
Moreover when ye fast, be not, as the hypocrites, of a sad countenance: for they disfigure their faces, that they may appear unto men to fast. Verily I say unto you, They have their reward.

Matthew 17:21
Howbeit this kind goeth not out but by prayer and fasting.

Psalm 139:8
If I go up to the heavens, you are there; if I make my bed in the depths, you are there.

Act 2:4
And they were all filled with the Holy Ghost, and began to speak with other tongues, as the Spirit gave them utterance.

Act 2:35
Until I make thy foes thy footstool.

Act 2:38
Then Peter said unto them, Repent, and be baptized every one of you in the name of Jesus Christ for the remission of sins, and ye shall receive the gift of the Holy Ghost.

Philippines 4:13
I can do all things through Christ which strengtheneth me.

1 Timothy 1:7
Desiring to be teachers of the law; understanding neither what they say, nor whereof they affirm.

John 4: 14
But whosoever drinketh of the water that I shall give him shall never thirst; but the water that I shall give him shall be in him a well of water springing up into everlasting life.

Revelation 12:11
And they overcame him by the blood of the Lamb, and by the word of their testimony; and they loved not their lives unto the death.

2 Corinthians 1:20
For all the promises of God in him are yea, and in him Amen, unto the glory of God by us.

Romans 2:11
For God does not show favoritism.

.

Malachi 3:10
Bring the whole tithe into the storehouse, that there may be food in my house. Test me in this," says the LORD Almighty, "and see if I will not throw open the floodgates of heaven and pour out so much blessing that there will not be room enough to store it

Revelation 22:13
I am the Alpha and the Omega, the First and the Last, the Beginning and the End

Proverbs 18:22
He who finds a wife finds what is good and receives favor from the LORD.

Deuteronomy 31:6
Be strong and courageous. Do not be afraid or terrified because of them, for the LORD your God goes with you; he will never leave you nor forsake you

Matthew 18:18
Truly I tell you, whatever you bind on earth will be[a] bound in heaven, and whatever you loose on earth will be[b] loosed in heaven.

THANK YOU FOR YOUR SUPPORT!

- ANDREA SYLVE
- BERTHA CHARGOIS
- BIANCA CARRIER
- BIRDIA SESSUM
- BRENDA MALBROUGH
- BRITTNEY SESSUM
- CHRISTINA LEDAY
- CICELY GABRIEL
- CRYSTAL DAIGLE
- DAMETRIA LIPFORD
- DANIELLE GUILLORY
- DEVIN THOMAS
- ELIZABETH PHYSICIAN
- JANICE FREEMAN
- JASMINE JOHNSON
- JILLIAN HAMILTON
- LOIS RHODES

THANK YOU FOR YOUR SUPPORT!

Judy Smith
Katie Clay
Kim Sessum
Kimberly Paddio
Layota Rideaux
Loren Lewis
Malcolm Chenier
Mary Physician
Nicole Duplechain
Nicole Handy
Rachel Marie Richard
Raven Bellard
Ro Brooks
Sabrina Hernandez
Shantel Small
Shelia Chavis
Tonya Sacha
Thomas Carrier

Cute Self-Publishing and Writing Consultation Congratulates Katina Moore Chachere on publishing her first book. To God be the Glory!!!

ABOUT THE AUTHOR

Katina Moore Chachere born and raised in Rayne LA. She is married to Tamarcus. Together, they have two children - one son and one daughter and two grandchildren. Katina is a prayer warrior. She is the founder of *"Ministry Depot."* This *Ministry Depot* is designed to meet the needs of the community where she hosts a weekly prayer gathering. *"Breaking Through Katina Chachere"* airs Wednesday 2 PM on Facebook Live. She is a ministry leader of "Proverbs 31 Woman" prayer ministry started after the COVID-19 pandemic. The 4th of seven children, Katina is a student of the guitar a gift she inherited from her dad. She supports her husband, Tamarcus, in his big rig trucking business – Boyd Bros.

Follow Katina on all social media platforms Breaking Through Katina Chachere. Her goal is to make disciples of Jesus Christ.

Katina Moore Chachere's *"Shame on You Breakthrough"* shares the compelling testimony of deliverance from a substance use disorder that includes a pill addiction. Katina overcame the shame of childhood trauma, that of being molested, only to find herself in the shame of addiction. She later learned and understood the shame was not reaching out to GOD FIRST. Through her knowledge, Katina takes her reader on a step-by-step journey as she prayed and fasted her way out of addiction. As a result of reading *"Shame on You Breakthrough,"* the reader will gain the necessary tools to reach out to the one who can break any stronghold in our lives – GOD. You will receive the deliverance by the mighty name of Jesus Christ, healing, and breakthrough you need.

For more information on *Shame on You Breakthrough*, or to contact the author:

Email: Tinamoechachere@gmail.com

Facebook: Breaking Through Katina Chachere

Instagram: Breaking Through Katina

www.ingramcontent.com/pod-product-compliance
Lightning Source LLC
Chambersburg PA
CBHW070107100426
42743CB00012B/2669